A Teacher's Guide

To Using
The Creative Curriculum®
Developmental Continuum Assessment System

Diane Trister Dodge

Laura J. Colker

Cate Heroman

Teaching Strategies Inc.
Washington, DC

Editors: Toni Bickart, Rachel Friedlander Tickner
Design: Graves Fowler Associates

Copyright ©2001 Teaching Strategies, Inc.

Published by:
Teaching Strategies, Inc.
P.O. Box 42243
Washington, DC 20015
www.TeachingStrategies.com

Eighth Printing: 2008
Printed and bound in the United States

ISBN: 978-1-879537-54-5

Acknowledgments

The Creative Curriculum® Developmental Continuum for Ages 3–5 forms the core of this Toolkit. In 1998 we convened a group to review *The Creative Curriculum*'s child development goals and objectives. Special thanks to Dr. Carol Copple, who took a lead role in this effort. Derry G. Koralek, Monica Vacca, and Elizabeth Servideo also provided invaluable assistance in this task. We want to acknowledge Whit Hayslip, Coordinator of Infant and Preschool Programs, Division of Special Education, Los Angeles Unified School District and Karen Krische, program specialist, who arranged for a group of special education preschool teachers to work on the *Continuum* with Dr. M. Diane Klein, Chair of the Special Education Division at California State University, Los Angeles. This group developed the Forerunners, piloted the instrument in their classrooms, and generously shared their experiences. We also want to thank the Mesa Public Schools (Preschool Program), Arizona and the Summit Child Care Program, New Jersey for their help with an initial field test of the *Continuum*.

During 2000-2001, Dr. Martha Abbott-Shim of Quality Assist, Inc. conducted a study to determine the validity and reliability of *The Creative Curriculum Developmental Continuum*. Forty-one classrooms were involved in the reliability study including child care (43%), Head Start (31%), and public preschool (26%) programs. We thank the supervisors and teachers in the following programs: Summit Child Care Programs, Summit, NJ; Mesa Public Schools, Mesa, AZ; Salida Union School District Head Start, Modesto, CA; and five programs in Louisiana: Ascension Parish Head Start; Ouachita Parish School System, St. Tammany Parish School System, Lafourche Parish School System, and the Baton Rouge Country Day School. We also want to acknowledge the 40 early childhood experts who participated in the content validity study of the *Developmental Continuum*. This group included professors, trainers, directors, and teachers. Additional information on research involving *The Creative Curriculum* and *The Creative Curriculum Developmental Continuum* can be found on our web site: www.TeachingStrategies.com under "Research."

The *Toolkit* reflects the input of many colleagues at Teaching Strategies who helped refine the assessment tools. Toni Bickart, then editor-in-chief, improved many drafts and made sure that our instructions were clear and accurate. Doug Gritzmacher, then production coordinator, and Rachel Friedlander Tickner, editorial assistant, cheerfully revised many versions of the forms. Sharon Yandian, then director of training, and Fran Simon, then Web editor, offered thoughtful comments and feedback on the content. Larry Bram, then director of marketing, helped to propel the project forward. We are very grateful to have such a dedicated staff, committed to ensuring the highest quality products.

Table of Contents

Introduction

What does it mean to implement a curriculum? How do you plan for a group of children and for each child? How do you know that every child in your classroom is making progress? How do you demonstrate that your program is effective in helping children grow and learn?

These are critical questions for everyone involved in early childhood education: curriculum developers, teachers who implement the curriculum in their classrooms, administrators who are held accountable for positive outcomes, and parents who want to be sure their children are progressing. A critical factor in successfully implementing any developmentally appropriate curriculum and meeting the needs of every child is having in place an assessment system that reflects the curriculum's goals and objectives for children.

How Assessment and Curriculum Are Linked

Teachers are decision makers. You use a curriculum that is based on child development research—which tells you what to expect of children at a given stage of development—so that you can set up an environment and plan experiences that support children's growth and learning. In using that curriculum to guide your planning, you make decisions every day:

- Is our room arrangement making it easy for children to focus on an activity?

- Are the children able to make choices, and do they take care of materials?

- Is the daily schedule meeting the needs of the children for active and quiet times?

- How can we make transitions smoother?

- When is a good time to introduce new props in the block area?

- What are children interested in learning more about?

As a teacher, you also make countless decisions on a daily basis about individual children:

- Will it help Setsuko pay attention during story time if she sits near me?

- How can I help Malik learn how to make a friend?

- Leo falls apart at naptime every day. What can we do to make this period easier for him?

- Crystal is excited about her new puppy. How can we build on this new interest to promote her language and literacy skills?

- Devon has been building the same block structure for weeks. Is he stuck? How can I extend his interest in block building?

Assessment gives you the information you need to make these decisions about the program or about individual children. The more information you have, the better your decisions. Effective assessment requires:

- Understanding what you want children to learn—the curriculum goals and objectives.

- Knowing the developmental steps you can expect children to go through to accomplish each objective.

- Observing children each day and documenting what you see and hear.

- Collecting information about each child by talking with families and keeping samples and photographs of children's work over time.

- Summarizing what you learn about each child to share with families and planning together how best to support the child's learning.

The Creative Curriculum® for Preschool, published in 2002, includes *The Creative Curriculum Developmental Continuum for Ages 3–5* based on *The Creative Curriculum*'s goals and objectives. The *Continuum* provides teachers with a structure for observing children to plan for each child. Because early childhood programs have been mandated to show that all children are making progress and that the program is effective, we provide specific guidance to clarify the critical link between curriculum and assessment.

The initial result of our efforts was *The Creative Curriculum Developmental Continuum Assessment Toolkit*. We have since also developed CreativeCurriculum.net, the comprehensive, online subscription service described at www.CreativeCurriculum.net, and *The Expanded Forerunners of The Creative Curriculum Developmental Continuum for Ages 3–5*. Children identified with developmental delays or disabilities may require the use of *The Expanded Forerunners* to show progress at the Forerunner level. See Appendix B for an example.

Contents of the *Toolkit*

This *Toolkit* provides all the assessment materials you need to implement *The Creative Curriculum* in your preschool program.

- *A Teacher's Guide to Using The Creative Curriculum Developmental Continuum Assessment System* guides implementation of an assessment system linked directly to planning for a group and for each child.

- *The Creative Curriculum Developmental Continuum for Ages 3–5* shows the sequence of development for each of the 50 objectives.

- *The Creative Curriculum Goals and Objectives Poster* can be displayed in your classroom as a quick reference.

- The *Class Summary Worksheet* enables you to track and pinpoint progress for all of the children in your group on each of the 50 objectives.

- The *Individual Child Profile* is used to document each child's progress at three checkpoints during the year—fall, winter, and spring.

- *Child Progress and Planning Reports* are used to summarize a child's progress, gain input from the family, and plan together for the next steps.

Two other products are available separately. *The Expanded Forerunners* describe three sequential developmental steps within the Forerunner level of each objective. The *Individual Child Profile—Expanded Forerunners* is used to record a child's progress entirely within the Forerunner developmental step.

Overview of the *Teacher's Guide*

This *Teacher's Guide* helps you implement an ongoing assessment process as you use *The Creative Curriculum for Preschool*. It has the following chapters:

Curriculum Goals and Objectives: A Roadmap for Assessment

Goals and objectives are like a roadmap; they give you a direction for planning your program and a way to determine what children know and how they are progressing. Just as you read road signs or check a map when you take a trip to make sure you're on the right course, you also need a roadmap to chart each child's progress. In this chapter we introduce you to *The Creative Curriculum Developmental Continuum*, which shows the progress you can expect for 3- to 5-year-olds for each of the Curriculum's 50 objectives. It includes forerunners for children who may not be developing at a typical level but are still exhibiting strengths on which you can build.

Collecting Facts

The first phase in linking curriculum planning and assessment is collecting facts—learning as much as possible about each child. Ongoing observation is the primary way teachers collect objective facts. To help you remember and use what you learn from your observations, you need systems for documenting what you see. This part of *A Teacher's Guide* offers practical ideas for observing and documenting your observations and collecting samples of children's work over time to keep in their portfolios.

Analyzing and Evaluating Facts

Observation notes and samples of children's work reveal a wealth of information that needs to be organized, analyzed, and evaluated so you can determine exactly where a child is developmentally. For this stage in the assessment process, you have *The Creative Curriculum* Goals and Objectives at a Glance, the *Developmental Continuum*, the *Class Summary Worksheet*, and the *Individual Child Profile* forms.

Planning for Each Child and the Group

The information you now have that shows where each child is in relation to Curriculum objectives enables you to develop a plan to meet each child's needs. You review and summarize what you have learned about a child on the *Child Progress and Planning Report*, then meet with families to exchange information and plan the next steps. You also plan for your group of children by reviewing the information on the *Class Summary Worksheet* so you know how best to plan for the group while considering who may need more focused support and instruction in a given skill.

Using Technology to Analyze and Report on Group Progress

Who needs the information you have on children's progress? Families, teachers, administrators, and funders ask for documentation about program outcomes. Available separately from the *Toolkit* is *The Creative Curriculum Progress and Outcomes Reporting Tool* software (CC-PORT™). This package enables programs to generate reports that summarize the progress of groups of children in multiple classrooms and at multiple sites. With these reports you can evaluate program effectiveness and plan accordingly. Another option is CreativeCurriculum.net, the comprehensive, online subscription service for recording and reporting information, planning, and sharing information about a child with the family. For more information, visit www.CreativeCurriculum.net.

The following chart illustrates the ongoing relationship between assessment and curriculum.

Linking Curriculum and Assessment—The Ongoing Cycle

Planning for Assessment

- Become familiar with *The Creative Curriculum® Developmental Continuum*
- Set up a systematic way to observe, document, and organize your notes
- Set up a portfolio for each child

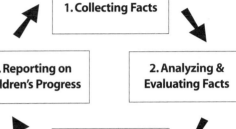

1. Collecting Facts

Observe and document children's learning

- Observe children with curriculum objectives in mind
- Document what you see and hear
- Collect samples of children's work over time for portfolios

2. Analyzing & Evaluating Facts

Analyze facts

- Sort observation notes by developmental area for each child
- Label each note and work sample with the number of each objective that applies to the observation

Evaluate children's progress

- Review observation notes and portfolio items
- Use the *Developmental Continuum* to identify what step each child has reached for each of the 50 objectives
- Use the *Class Summary Worksheet* to keep track of children's progress from checkpoint to checkpoint
- Enter information on the *Individual Child Profile* at each checkpoint

3. Planning for Each Child & the Group

Plan for each child

- Summarize each child's progress on the *Child Progress and Planning Report*
- Meet with families to share information and jointly plan next steps
- Implement your plan and continue to observe the child's progress

Plan for the group

- Reflect on the progress of your group based on the *Class Summary Worksheet*
- Decide which objectives to target for the whole group and for selected children
- Plan strategies to support children's learning—whole group, small group activities
- Implement your plan and continue to observe children's progress

4. Reporting on Children's Progress

- Generate reports as needed
- Identify aspects of the program that need strengthening and develop a program improvement plan

---

 ©2004 Teaching Strategies, Inc., PO Box 42243, Washington, DC 20015; www.TeachingStrategies.com

1. Curriculum Goals and Objectives: A Roadmap for Assessment

Goals and objectives are the roadmap of a preschool curriculum. They provide a direction for planning and an organizational structure for determining what each child knows and how each child is developing. The goals of a preschool curriculum should address all aspects of development:

- *Social/Emotional Development:* children's feelings about themselves, the development of responsibility, and their ability to relate positively to others.

- *Physical Development:* children's gross and fine motor development.

- *Cognitive Development:* children's thinking skills—the development of logical and symbolic thinking, problem-solving skills, and approaches to learning.

- *Language Development:* children's ability to communicate through words, both spoken and written.

For an overview of the 10 goals and 50 objectives, see *The Creative Curriculum* Goals and Objectives at a Glance (Appendix A).

Looking at Objectives on a Continuum

The Creative Curriculum Developmental Continuum shows the developmental steps for each of the Curriculum objectives for children ages 3–5, including children who may not be at a typical level. *The Expanded Forerunners* provide a more in-depth picture for children whose development is solidly at the Forerunner level in multiple objectives or developmental areas. Children don't accomplish a particular skill all at once. There is a sequence of steps you can expect them to go through as they progress toward mastering an objective. Having a way to determine where each child is in relation to curriculum goals and objectives enables you to decide what specific support and what kinds of experiences will enable each child to develop and learn—at any level.

The figure that follows illustrates the different components of the *Continuum*.

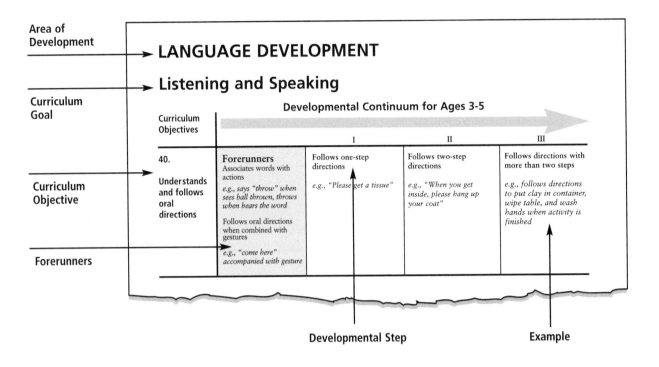

The three non-shaded boxes below the long gray arrow (labeled steps I, II, and III) represent the expected developmental steps in the preschool years (children ages 3 to 5). Each box describes a particular point in skill development. Because children develop at very different rates, these boxes do **not** represent a specific age; rather, they show the expected **developmental steps** in mastering the objective. Step I, therefore, approximates a beginning level of development. For objective 40, Understands and follows oral directions, step I reads "Follows one-step directions." To give you a picture of what this might look like in real life, we provide an **example:** *Please get a tissue.*

In step II, we offer the next level in acquiring this skill: "Follows two-step directions given." An example might be a child who can carry out this oral direction: *When you get inside, please hang up your coat.*

Step III represents a higher level of skill development: "Follows directions with more than two steps." An example that illustrates this step is, *Follows directions to put clay in container, wipe table, and wash hands when activity is finished.*

Keep in mind that because all of the examples presented in the *Continuum* are **sample** behaviors, you may or may not observe these actual behaviors. Children demonstrate their mastery of skills in a variety of ways.

Including All Children

The skills and stages identified in steps I, II, and III will cover most of the children in your program. However, there may be children who go beyond the scope of this *Continuum*, and others whose development in one or more areas is not at a typical level. Some of these children may have special education needs or a diagnosed disability. Over the past 30 years, with federal law's emphasis on educating children in the "least restrictive environment" (as mandated by the Individuals with Disabilities Education Act of 1997), more children with disabilities are joining their non-disabled peers in preschool. There also may be some children who, because of lack of experience, may not have had an opportunity to develop a particular skill. For example, a child who has never had a crayon or marker in his hand may be in the very early stages of writing.

The *Continuum* gives you a way of identifying children who are not yet at the beginning level of typical preschool development, as indicated by step I. These children do, however, show beginning evidence of developing the skills and knowledge involved—a strength on which to build. Thus we offer some possible **forerunner** skills. In the example we've been using (objective 40, "Understands and follows oral directions"), forerunner skills include:

- associates words with actions (e.g., says "throw" when sees ball thrown, throws ball when hears the word)

- follows oral directions when combined with gestures (e.g., "come here" accompanied with gesture)

These forerunners are examples of the many possible emergent skills a child might exhibit. Before achieving a skill that is typical of 3- to 5-year-olds, children with delays will display a wide range of emerging behaviors. You are likely to observe forerunner skills that either precede or follow the ones we have included in the *Continuum*. The forerunners we have listed do not represent a timeline; they are *examples* of possible skills and behaviors on which you can build when planning for children.

Including this forerunner cell supports a belief that underlies *The Creative Curriculum*: all children bring with them strengths and abilities on which you can build. (See *The Expanded Forerunners* if you need more assessment guidelines for children who are not developing typically.)

The Benefits of a Continuum

The Creative Curriculum Developmental Continuum can become an invaluable tool for planning your program and individualizing *The Creative Curriculum* for each child.

- It breaks down each objective so you can have realistic expectations as you plan.

- It helps you to observe and plan for all children in your program, including those who may not be developing typically, and note their progress over time.

- It fosters a positive approach to teaching children—looking at their strengths and thinking about what comes next, rather than recording their weaknesses.

- It gives you a wealth of information to share with families that will reassure them about their child's progress as a learner.

The Creative Curriculum Goals and Objectives

The Developmental Continuum addresses four areas of development—social/emotional, physical, cognitive, and language. Under these four areas there are 10 goals and 50 objectives.

Social/Emotional Development

The preschool years are a prime time for developing the social and emotional skills essential to children's well-being and success, in school and in life. With the current focus on readiness, accountability, and high standards, there is always a danger that programs will push inappropriate academic skills and ignore other significant aspects of development.

A Good Beginning: Sending America's Children to School with the Social and Emotional Competence They Need to Succeed (The Child Mental Health Foundations and Agencies Network 2000, 7) confirms scientific evidence that social and emotional readiness is critical to a successful kindergarten transition, early school success, and even later accomplishments in the workplace. The report describes a child who is socially and emotionally ready for school as having these characteristics:

- is confident, friendly, has developed or will be able to develop good relationships with peers

- is able to concentrate on and persist at challenging tasks

- is able to effectively communicate frustrations, anger, and joy

- is able to listen to instructions and be attentive

The skills related to these characteristics can be taught and nurtured most effectively when children are young.

Strategies for achieving social and emotional objectives are embedded throughout *The Creative Curriculum*. We have organized the objectives under three goals.

- *Sense of self.* This refers to how children feel accepted and valued by the people who are most important to them.

- *Responsibility for self and others.* This goal is about developing habits and character traits such as responsibility, independence, and self-direction, and following rules and routines.

- *Prosocial behavior.* This includes traits that will help children get along in the world, such as empathy, sharing, and taking turns.

Sense of Self

Curriculum Objectives	Developmental Continuum for Ages 3-5			
		I	II	III
1. **Shows ability to adjust to new situations**	**Forerunners** Interacts with teachers when family member is nearby Is able to move away from family member; checks back occasionally ("social referencing")	Treats arrival and departure as routine parts of the day e.g., says good-bye to family members without undue stress; accepts comfort from teacher	Accepts changes in daily schedules and routines e.g., eagerly participates in a field trip; accepts visitors to classroom	Functions with increasing independence in school e.g., readily goes to other parts of the building for scheduled activities; willingly delivers a message from classroom teacher to the office
2. **Demonstrates appropriate trust in adults**	**Forerunners** Seeks to be near trusted adult as a "safe haven" Makes visual or physical contact with trusted adult for reassurance	Shows confidence in parents' and teachers' abilities to keep him/her safe and healthy e.g., explores the indoor and outdoor environments without being fearful; summons adult when assistance is needed	Regards parents and teachers as resources and positive role models e.g., imitates parents going to work or at home during dramatic play; asks teacher's advice on how to saw a piece of wood in half	Knows the difference between adults who can help (family members, friends, staff) and those who may not (strangers) e.g., knows who is allowed to give her medicine; talks about why children shouldn't go anywhere with strangers
3. **Recognizes own feelings and manages them appropriately**	**Forerunners** Cries to express displeasure Uses facial expressions to communicate feelings e.g., nods when asked if he is feeling sad	Identifies and labels own feelings e.g., says, "I'm mad at you"; "I really want to paint today"	Is able to describe feelings and their causes e.g., says, "I'm excited because my dad is coming home"; "I'm mad because they won't let me play with them"	Is increasingly able to manage own feelings e.g., calms self down when angry and uses words to explain why; chooses to go to a quiet area to be alone when upset

4. **Stands up for rights**	**Forerunners** Protests when slighted or wronged by crying or yelling Grabs or pushes when seeking a desired toy	Physically or verbally asserts needs and desires *e.g., continues to hold classroom pet another child wants; lets teacher know if another child refuses to give anyone a turn on the ride-on truck*	Asserts own needs and desires verbally without being aggressive *e.g., says, "It's my turn now" when sand timer runs out; tells friend who asks to paint at the easel, "I'm not done," and continues working*	Takes action to avoid possible disputes over rights *e.g., puts up "Do not knock down" sign in front of block structure; divides sandbox into area for himself and peer*

Responsibility for Self and Others

Curriculum Objectives	**Developmental Continuum for Ages 3-5**		
	I	II	III
5. **Demonstrates self-direction and independence**	**Forerunners** Purposefully indicates needs or wants (may be nonverbal) Selects toy or activity; plays briefly	Chooses and becomes involved in one activity out of several options *e.g., during free play decides to play with giant dominoes on floor in toys and games area; after waking up from nap, takes book from shelf in library area and looks at it*	Completes multiple tasks in a project of own choosing with some adult assistance *e.g., makes a collage: collects materials, glue, paper, and scissors and works until done; builds a zoo with blocks, animal and people props, and cars*	Carves out and completes own task without adult assistance *e.g., draws one section of mural without intruding on other sections; makes a book about family trip that includes 5 pictures in sequence*
6. **Takes responsibility for own well-being**	**Forerunners** Allows adult to attend to personal needs such as dressing or washing hands without resistance Uses self-help skills with adult assistance such as brushing teeth or putting on coat with help	Uses self-help skills with occasional reminders *e.g., tries new foods when encouraged by teacher; washes hands with soap and water following procedures taught*	Uses self-help skills and participates in chores without reminders *e.g., goes to get a sponge after spilling juice; helps throw away trash after a picnic*	Understands the importance of self-help skills and their role in healthy living *e.g., tries new foods and talks about what's good for you; knows why it's important to wash hands and brush teeth*
7. **Respects and cares for classroom environment and materials**	**Forerunners** Engages with/explores materials for brief periods of time with adult assistance or independently Participates in clean-up routines when asked	Uses materials in appropriate ways *e.g., paints at easel; turns pages in book carefully without tearing*	Puts away used materials before starting another activity *e.g., shuts off the tape recorder before leaving the listening center; returns puzzle to shelf*	Begins to take responsibility for care of the classroom environment *e.g., gets broom and dust pan to help remove sand; pitches in willingly to move furniture to clear a group area*

Responsibility for Self and Others (continued)

8. Follows classroom routines	**Forerunners** Allows adult to move him/her through routines Follows classroom routines with assistance such as reminders, picture cues, or physical help	Participates in classroom activities (e.g., circle time, clean-up, napping, toileting, eating, etc.) with prompting *e.g., after cleaning up, goes to rug for circle time when the teacher strums the autoharp*	Understands and follows classroom procedures without prompting *e.g., goes to wash hands and brush teeth after lunch*	Follows and understands the purpose of classroom procedures *e.g., tells peer that he can't eat lunch until he's washed his hands*
9. Follows classroom rules	**Forerunners** Follows simple directions and limits when told by an adult Follows classroom rules with assistance such as reminders, picture cues, or physical help	Follows classroom rules with reminders *e.g., responds positively to guidance such as "speak with your indoor voice"*	Understands and follows classroom rules without reminders *e.g., returns puzzles to shelf before leaving the table area*	Follows and understands reasons for classroom rules *e.g., tells friend to put artwork on shelf so it will be safe; reminds peer not to run in classroom so that no one will get hurt*

Prosocial Behavior

Curriculum Objectives	Developmental Continuum for Ages 3-5		
	I	II	III
10. Plays well with other children	**Forerunners** Tolerates being physically near others Plays alongside another child Enjoys simple back and forth games such as hide and seek	Works/plays cooperatively with one other child *e.g., draws or paints beside peer, making occasional comments; has a pretend phone conversation with another child*	Successfully enters a group and plays cooperatively *e.g., joins other children caring for babies in dramatic play center; plans with peers what they will need to set up a class restaurant*	Maintains an ongoing friendship with at least one other child *e.g., says, "We're friends again, right?" after working through a conflict; talks about another child as "my best friend"*
11. Recognizes the feelings of others and responds appropriately	**Forerunners** Notices expressions of feelings in others *e.g., looks or reacts by crying or laughing* Imitates other children's expressions of feelings	Is aware of other children's feelings and often responds in a like manner *e.g., laughs or smiles when others are happy; says a child is sad because her mom left*	Shows increasing awareness that people may have different feelings about the same situation *e.g., says that another child is afraid of thunder but, "I'm not"; acts out role of angry parent during pretend play*	Recognizes what another person might need or want *e.g., brings a book on trucks to show a child who loves trucks; helps a friend who is having difficulty opening a milk carton*

12. Shares and respects the rights of others	**Forerunners** Plays alongside another child using same or similar materials with adult assistance Plays alongside another child using same or similar materials without conflict	With prompts, shares or takes turns with others *e.g., allows sand timer to regulate turns with favorite toys; complies with teacher's request to let another child have a turn on the tricycle*	Shares toys or allows turn in response to another child's request *e.g., appropriately occupies self while waiting for others to leave swings without crying or demanding a turn; plays at sand table without grabbing items being used by others*	Shares and defends the rights of others to a turn *e.g., reminds child who doesn't want to relinquish a turn that it is another child's turn; asks teacher to intervene when two children begin to fight over a toy*
13. Uses thinking skills to resolve conflicts	**Forerunners** Accepts adult solution to resolve a conflict Seeks adult assistance to resolve a conflict *e.g., cries, approaches adult, or asks for help*	Accepts compromise when suggested by peer or teacher *e.g., agrees to play with another toy while waiting for a turn; goes to "peace table" with teacher and peer to solve a problem*	Suggests a solution to solve a problem; seeks adult assistance when needed *e.g., suggests trading one toy for another; asks teacher to make a waiting list for the water table*	Engages in a process of negotiation to reach a compromise *e.g., works out roles for a dramatic play episode; suggests going to the "peace table" to work out a problem*

Physical Development

Children's physical development is sometimes taken for granted in early childhood. We assume children will progress though a predictable sequence of stages and acquire certain skills. However, physical development is far too important to leave to chance.

Physical skills are important in their own right and for future tasks in reading, writing, scientific explorations, and math. For example, when children string beads, line up shells, or use the zipper on a self-help frame, they are refining their eye-hand coordination, fine motor skills, and sense of directionality.

Physical development also affects social/emotional development. As children learn what their bodies can do, they gain self-confidence. The more they can do, the more willingly they try new and increasingly challenging tasks. This positive attitude means that children are more willing to try out new physical skills without fear of failure. This increased self-confidence positively influences their attitude toward learning in other areas of development.

The benefits of promoting physical skills are well documented. The Surgeon General's *Report on Physical Activity and Health* (1996) states that physical activity contributes significantly to personal health and well-being. Physical education in the early grades contributes to children's academic achievement, general health, self-esteem, stress management, and social development. And we know from brain research that movement literally "wakes up" the brain.

For these reasons, *The Creative Curriculum* goals and objectives guide teachers in providing children with opportunities each day to move skillfully, manipulate objects, balance and control their bodies, and refine small muscle skills. We have organized the objectives for physical development into two broad goals.

- *Gross motor* development involves the movements controlled by the body's large muscles. It includes how children move from one place to another by running, jumping, hopping, galloping, and skipping. This goal also addresses gross motor manipulative skills such as throwing, kicking, and catching. Balance and stability are also important aspects of gross motor development.

- *Fine motor* development focuses on the control, coordination, and dexterity of the small muscles in the hands. As these fine muscles develop, children will be increasingly able to perform simple self-help skills and manipulate objects such as scissors and writing tools. Fine motor skills generally lag behind gross motor development.

Gross Motor

Curriculum Objectives	Developmental Continuum for Ages 3-5			
		I	II	III
14. **Demonstrates basic locomotor skills (running, jumping, hopping, galloping)**	**Forerunners** Walks with assistance Runs, sometimes falls Jumps and hops with hand held	Moves with direction and beginning coordination *e.g., runs avoiding obstacles; jumps forward, may lead with one foot; hops in place once or twice*	Moves with direction and increasing coordination *e.g., runs moving arms and legs; does a running jump with both feet; attempts to skip, often reverting to galloping*	Moves with direction and refined coordination *e.g., runs quickly changing directions, starting and stopping; jumps forward from standing position; gallops smoothly*
15. **Shows balance while moving**	**Forerunners** Walks on toes Easily stops, starts, changes direction, avoids obstacles Walks forward straddling line	Attempts to walk along a line, stepping off occasionally	Walks along wide beam such as edge of sandbox	Walks forward easily, and backward with effort, along a wide beam

16. Climbs up and down	**Forerunners** Crawls up stairs on own Walks up stairs with hand held Climbs a short, wide ladder with support from adult	Climbs a short, wide ladder	Climbs up and down stairs and ladders, and around obstacles	Climbs and plays easily on ramps, stairs, ladders, or sliding boards
17. Pedals and steers a tricycle (or other wheeled vehicle)	**Forerunners** Sits on tricycle or other riding toy, pushing forward/backward with feet not using pedals Pedals tricycle, difficulty with steering	Pedals in forward direction, steering around wide corners	Pedals and steers around obstacles and sharp corners	Rides with speed and control
18. Demonstrates throwing, kicking, and catching skills	**Forerunners** Hurls beanbag or ball Sits on floor and traps a rolled ball with arms and body Kicks a ball a short distance with hand held to maintain balance	Throws, catches, and kicks objects with somewhat awkward movements *e.g., throws ball with both hands; catches a large ball against body; kicks ball from standing position*	Throws, catches, and kicks with increasing control *e.g., throws ball overhand several feet toward target; catches bounced ball; moves toward ball and kicks*	Throws and kicks at target and catches with increasing accuracy *e.g., throws object with smooth overhand motion; catches object with elbows bent; kicks ball with fluid motion*

Fine Motor

Curriculum Objectives	**Developmental Continuum for Ages 3-5**		
	I	II	III
19. Controls small muscles in hands	**Forerunners** Uses self-help skills such as: finger feeds self; removes shoes/socks; washes hands with assistance Drops objects into container Touches thumb to finger to pick up object	Manipulates objects with hands *e.g., places large pegs in pegboard; buttons large buttons on own clothes; uses scissors to make snips*	Manipulates smaller objects with increasing control *e.g., eats with a fork; inserts and removes small pegs in pegboard; squeezes clothespin to hang painting; cuts with scissors along a straight or slightly curved line*	Manipulates a variety of objects requiring increased coordination *e.g., creates recognizable objects with clay; buttons, zips, and sometimes ties; cuts with scissors along lines, turning corners; cuts simple shapes out of paper*

Fine Motor (continued)

20. Coordinates eye-hand movement	**Forerunners** Removes pegs from pegboard Opens a board book and turns a page Puts one block on top of another, holding the base block	Performs simple manipulations *e.g., makes a necklace with a string and large beads; rolls and pounds playdough; places pegs in pegboard*	Performs simple manipulations with increasing control *e.g., makes a necklace using small beads; pours water into a funnel*	Manipulates materials in a purposeful way, planning and attending to detail *e.g., strings a variety of small objects (straws, buttons, etc.); using table blocks, creates a tall structure that balances; completes 8-piece puzzle*
21. Uses tools for writing and drawing	**Forerunners** Holds large writing tool and marks with it Holds marker in palmar grasp and scribbles	Holds a marker or crayon with thumb and two fingers; makes simple strokes	Makes several basic strokes or figures; draws some recognizable objects	Copies and draws simple shapes, letters, and words including name

Cognitive Development

Cognitive development is the process of learning to think and reason. Preschool-age children are developing cognitive skills that prepare them for content work in all of the disciplines. They are becoming skilled observers and questioners and learning how to organize and represent new information.

In reviewing standards in all of the content areas, you will find a common thread. Cognitive or thinking skills are embedded within literacy, mathematics, science, social studies, the arts, and technology. Most of these standards documents refer to them as "process skills." As you read through the list of goals and objectives for cognitive development, think about how each might be applied in different academic areas. For example, the objective, "Explores cause and effect," can be observed in many different ways:

- "If the big, bad wolf goes down the chimney, he's going to get burned!" (Literacy)
- "If you give me one more cookie, I'll have two all together." (Math)
- "We forgot to water our plant and it died." (Science)
- "If we put a letter in the mailbox, the postal carrier will deliver it." (Social Studies)
- "If you add too much water to the paint, it will run down the paper." (The Arts)

Children's cognitive development is more than memorizing facts. In the early childhood years, children are not only learning knowledge, skills, and concepts, but also acquiring the "learning to learn" skills that are so important for future learning. We have divided cognitive development into three goals.

- *Learning and problem solving*. This goal involves helping children to be thoughtful about how they use information, resources, and materials. They think about their ideas, make predictions, and test possible solutions. Approaches to learning, such as curiosity, persistence, and applying knowledge, take learning to a higher level beyond just learning facts.

- *Logical thinking*. This goal is about helping children to make sense of the information they are gathering. They compare, contrast, sort, classify, count, measure, and recognize patterns to gain a deeper understanding of the concepts they are learning.

- *Representation and symbolic thinking*. This goal focuses on how children use symbols in thought. A symbol stands for something else. Symbols can be objects (a pot used as a drum), people (pretending to be a mommy), or representations through drawings. Graphs to represent numbers or written words that represent spoken words are also examples of representation and symbolic thinking.

Learning and Problem Solving

Curriculum Objectives	Developmental Continuum for Ages 3-5			
		I	II	III
22. **Observes objects and events with curiosity**	**Forerunners** Looks at and touches object presented by an adult or another child Explores materials in the environment *e.g., touching, looking, smelling, mouthing, listening, playing*	Examines with attention to detail, noticing attributes of objects *e.g., points out stripes on caterpillar; notices it gets darker when the sun goes behind a cloud; points out changes in animals or plants in room*	Notices and/or asks questions about similarities and differences *e.g., points out that two trucks are the same size; asks why the leaves fall off the trees*	Observes attentively and seeks relevant information *e.g., describes key features of different models of cars (such as logos, number of doors, type of license plate); investigates which objects will sink and which will float*
23. **Approaches problems flexibly**	**Forerunners** Imitates adult or peer in solving problems Repeats and persists in trial and error approach	Finds multiple uses for classroom objects *e.g., uses wooden blocks as musical instruments; strings wooden beads into necklace for dress-up*	Experiments with materials in new ways when first way doesn't work *e.g., when playdough recipe produces sticky dough, asks for more flour; fills plastic bottle with water to make it sink*	Finds alternative solutions to problems *e.g., suggests using block as doorstop when classroom doorstop disappears; offers to swap trike for riding toy she wants and then adds fire-fighter hat to the bargain*

Learning and Problem Solving *(continued)*

24. **Shows persistence in approaching tasks**	**Forerunners** Remains engaged in a task for short periods with assistance Stays involved in self-selected activity such as playing with playdough for short periods	Sees simple tasks through to completion *e.g., puts toys away before going on to next activity; completes 5-piece puzzle*	Continues to work on task even when encountering difficulties *e.g., rebuilds block tower when it tumbles; keeps trying different puzzle pieces when pieces aren't fitting together*	Works on task over time, leaving and returning to complete it *e.g., continues to work on Lego structure over 3-day period; creates grocery store out of hollow blocks, adding more detail each day, and involves other children in playing grocery*
25. **Explores cause and effect**	**Forerunners** Notices an effect *e.g., shows pleasure in turning light switch on and off, wants to do it again; repeatedly stacks blocks and watches them fall* Looks for something when it is out of sight	Notices and comments on effect *e.g., while shaking a jar of water says, "Look at the bubbles when I do this"; after spinning around and stopping says, "Spinning makes the room look like it's moving up and down"*	Wonders "what will happen if" and tests out possibilities *e.g., blows into cardboard tubes of different sizes to hear if different sounds are made; changes the incline of a board to make cars slide down faster*	Explains plans for testing cause and effect, and tries out ideas *e.g., places pennies one by one in 2 floating boats ("I'm seeing which boat sinks first"); mixes gray paint to match another batch ("Let's put in one drop of white at a time 'til it's right")*
26. **Applies knowledge or experience to a new context**	**Forerunners** Follows familiar self-help routines at school (toileting, eating)—may need assistance	Draws on everyday experiences and applies this knowledge to similar situations *e.g., washes hands after playing at sand table; rocks baby doll in arms*	Applies new information or vocabulary to an activity or interaction *e.g., comments, "We're bouncing like Tigger" when jumping up and down with peer; uses traffic-directing signals after seeing a police officer demonstrate them*	Generates a rule, strategy, or idea from one learning experience and applies it in a new context *e.g., after learning to access one computer program by clicking on icons, uses similar procedures to access others; suggests voting to resolve a classroom issue*

Logical Thinking

Developmental Continuum for Ages 3-5

Curriculum Objectives	Forerunners	I	II	III
27. **Classifies objects**	**Forerunners** Finds two objects that are the same and comments or puts them together Groups similar kinds of toys together such as cars, blocks, or dolls	Sorts objects by one property such as size, shape, color, or use *e.g., sorts pebbles into three buckets by color; puts square block with other square blocks*	Sorts a group of objects by one property and then by another *e.g., collects leaves and sorts by size and then by color; puts self in group wearing shoes that tie and then in group with blue shoes*	Sorts objects into groups/subgroups and can state reason *e.g., sorts stickers into four piles ("Here are the stars that are silver and gold, and here are circles, silver and gold"); piles animals and then divides them into zoo and farm animals*
28. **Compares/ measures**	**Forerunners** Notices something new or different *e.g., a new classmate or a new toy on the shelf* Notices similarities of objects *e.g., "We have the same shoes"*	Notices similarities and differences *e.g., states, "The rose is the only flower in our garden that smells"; "I can run fast in my new shoes"*	Uses comparative words related to number, size, shape, texture, weight, color, speed, volume *e.g., "This bucket is heavier than that one"; "Now the music is going faster"*	Understands/uses measurement words and some standard measurement tools *e.g., uses unit blocks to measure length of rug; "We need 2 cups of flour and 1 cup of salt to make dough"*
29. **Arranges objects in a series**	**Forerunners** Uses self-correcting toys such as form boards and graduated stacking rings Sorts by one attribute *e.g., big blocks and little blocks*	Notices when one object in a series is out of place *e.g., removes the one measuring spoon out of place in a line and tries to put it in right place*	Figures out a logical order for a group of objects *e.g., makes necklace of graduated wooden beads; arranges magazine pictures of faces from nicest expression to meanest*	Through trial and error, arranges objects along a continuum according to two or more physical features *e.g., lines up bottle caps by height and width; sorts playdough cookies by size, color, and shape*
30. **Recognizes patterns and can repeat them**	**Forerunners** Completes a sentence that repeats in a familiar story Hums, sings, or responds to a chorus that repeats in a familiar song Completes a simple form board	Notices and recreates simple patterns with objects *e.g., makes a row of blocks alternating in size (big-small-big-small); strings beads in repeating patterns of 2 colors*	Extends patterns or creates simple patterns of own design *e.g., makes necklace of beads in which a sequence of 2 or more colors is repeated; continues block pattern of 2 colors*	Creates complex patterns of own design or by copying *e.g., imitates hand-clapping pattern (long clap followed by 3 short claps); designs a 3-color pattern using colored inch cubes and repeats it across the table*

Logical Thinking *(continued)*

31.	Forerunners	Demonstrates understanding of the present and may refer to past and future	Uses past and future tenses and time words appropriately	Associates events with time-related concepts
Shows awareness of time concepts and sequence	Follows steps in simple routine such as in dressing or at naptime Demonstrates understanding of what comes next in daily schedule *e.g., goes to the table anticipating mealtime*	*e.g., responds appropriately when asked, "What did you do this morning?"; talks about, "Later, when Mom comes to pick me up"*	*e.g., talks about tomorrow, yesterday, last week; says, "After work time, we go outside"*	*e.g., "Tomorrow is Saturday so there's no school"; "My birthday was last week"; "I go to bed at night"*
32.	Forerunners	Shows comprehension of basic positional words and concepts	Understands and uses positional words correctly	Shows understanding that positional relationships vary with one's perspective
Shows awareness of position in space	Moves objects from one container to another Follows simple positional directions with assistance *e.g., puts paper in trash can*	*e.g., puts object in, on, under, on top of, or next to another object as requested*	*e.g., "Come sit near me"; "The fish food goes on the top shelf"*	*e.g., turns lotto card around so player opposite him can see it right side up; "I can reach the ring when I'm on the top step, but from here it's too far"*
33.	Forerunners	Matches pairs of objects in one-to-one correspondence	Places objects in one-to-one correspondence with another set	Uses one-to-one correspondence as a way to compare two sets
Uses one-to-one correspondence	Places an object in each designated space *e.g., puts a peg doll in each hole in a toy bus*	*e.g., searches through dress-ups to find two shoes for her feet*	*e.g., lines up brushes to make sure there is one for each jar of paint; goes around the table placing one cup at each child's place*	*e.g., lines up cubes across from a friend's row to determine who has more; puts one rider next to each horse saying, "Are there enough horses for all the cowboys?"*
34.	Forerunners	Imitates counting behavior using number names (may not always say one number per item or get the sequence right)	Counts correctly up to 5 or so using one number for each object (may not always keep track of what has or has not been counted)	Counts to 10 or so connecting number words and symbols to the objects counted and knows that the last number describes the total
Uses numbers and counting	Understands the concept of "one" *e.g., picks up one object when asked* Understands the concept of more *e.g., picks up more of something when directed, or asks for more cheese*	*e.g., says the numbers from 1 to 5 while moving finger along a row of 8 items (not realizing that counting means one number per item)*	*e.g., counts out 5 pretzels taking one at a time from bowl; counts a collection of objects but may count an object more than one time*	*e.g., counts 8 bottle caps and says, "I have 8"; spins dial, then moves board game piece 6 spaces; draws 5 figures to show members of family*

Representation and Symbolic Thinking

Curriculum Objectives	Developmental Continuum for Ages 3-5			
		I	II	III
35. **Takes on pretend roles and situations**	**Forerunners** Imitates simple action *e.g., picks up phone; rocks baby* With adult or peer support, imitates routines *e.g., pretends to feed doll; pours coffee; pretends to sleep*	Performs and labels actions associated with a role *e.g., feeding the baby doll, says, "I'm the Mommy"; picks up phone and says, "Hello, is Suzie there?"*	Offers a play theme and scenario *e.g., "Let's play school"; while listening to doll's heartbeat with stethoscope announces that it's time to get the baby to the hospital*	Engages in elaborate and sustained role play *e.g., suggests a play theme and discusses who will do what; discusses with peer what to buy at grocery store, takes pocketbook and goes to grocery store*
36. **Makes believe with objects**	**Forerunners** Imitates adult's or another child's use of familiar objects *e.g., rocks doll; stirs the pot* Interacts appropriately with objects with adult or peer support *e.g., responds to pretend phone call by putting phone to ear and vocalizing*	Interacts appropriately with real objects or replicas in pretend play *e.g., uses a broken phone to make a pretend phone call; puts playdough cookies on little plastic plates*	Uses substitute object or gesture to represent real object *e.g., holds hand to ear and pretends to dial phone; builds a sand castle and puts shell on top for "satellite dish"*	Uses make-believe props in planned and sustained play *e.g., pretends with a peer to be garage mechanics working on cars made of blocks; sets up scene for playing school—students sit on pillows and teacher has a box for a desk*
37. **Makes and interprets representations**	**Forerunners** Labels scribbles as people or common objects Interacts and builds with blocks Begins to use descriptive labels in construction play *e.g., "house," "road"*	Draws or constructs and then names what it is *e.g., draws pictures with different shapes and says, "This is my house"; lines up unit blocks and says, "I'm making a road"*	Draws or builds a construction that represents something specific *e.g., makes a helicopter with Bristle Blocks; draws 6 legs on insect after looking at beetle*	Plans then creates increasingly elaborate representations *e.g., uses blocks to make a maze for the class gerbil; draws fire truck and includes many details*

Language Development

A solid foundation in language development gives children the skills they need to become successful learners. Children who have rich language and literacy experiences in preschool are more likely to develop strong language and literacy skills. These skills—the ability to listen, speak, read, and write—develop interdependently in children. Several important reports address this area of development.

In 1996, the International Reading Association and the National Council of Teachers of English developed the *Standards for English Language Arts*, which defined what children should know and be able to do in kindergarten through 12th grade. However, this left little guidance about what should happen in the preschool years.

Two years later, the National Research Council published a landmark document, *Preventing Reading Difficulties in Young Children* (1998), which provided more guidance in defining what language and literacy should look like in the early years, birth through third grade. Based on this document, the Council later published *Starting Out Right: A Guide to Promoting Children's Reading Success* (1999) to share the findings from its study of the research with teachers, parents, and child care providers.

In 1998, the International Reading Association (IRA) and the National Association for the Education of Young Children (NAEYC) jointly issued a document entitled, *Learning to Read and Write: Developmentally Appropriate Practices for Young Children* (Neuman, Copple, and Bredekamp 2000). This position statement on early literacy development provides teachers and policy makers with a set of principles and recommendations for children birth through age 8.

In 2000, the National Institute of Child Health and Human Development issued a report on how children learn to read, write, and understand written language: *Report of the National Reading Panel: Teaching Children to Read: An Evidence-Based Assessment of the Scientific Research Literature on Reading and Its Implications for Reading Instruction*. They identified the concepts children need to learn to become competent and confident readers and writers and the kinds of experiences that help them make progress.

To develop goals and objectives in this area of development, we used all these reports to identify what preschool children should learn and the developmental steps teachers can expect. We have grouped the language objectives into two goals.

- *Listening and speaking*. This goal involves spoken language. Having a large vocabulary, expressing oneself, understanding the oral speech of others, participating in a conversation, and using language to solve problems are important components of oral language development.

- *Reading and writing*. This goal involves helping children make sense of written language as they enjoy and value reading. Development in this area increases children's ability to handle books, understand the purpose of print and how it works, and comprehend a story. They gain knowledge of the alphabet and write letters and words during their play.

Listening and Speaking

Developmental Continuum for Ages 3-5

Curriculum Objectives	Forerunners	I	II	III
38. **Hears and discriminates the sounds of language**	**Forerunners** Notices sounds in the environment *e.g., pays attention to birds singing, sirens* Joins in nursery rhymes and songs	Plays with words, sounds, and rhymes *e.g., repeats songs, rhymes, and chants; says, "Oh you Silly Willy"*	Recognizes and invents rhymes and repetitive phrases; notices words that begin the same way *e.g., makes up silly rhymes ("Bo, Bo, Biddle, Bop"); says, "My name begins the same as popcorn and pig"*	Hears and repeats separate sounds in words; plays with sounds to create new words *e.g., claps hands 3 times when saying "Su-zan-na"; says, "Pass the bapkin [napkin]"*
39. **Expresses self using words and expanded sentences**	**Forerunners** Uses non-verbal gestures or single words to communicate *e.g., points to ball* Uses 2-word phrases *e.g., "All gone"; "Go out"*	Uses simple sentences (3-4 words) to express wants and needs *e.g., "I want the trike"*	Uses longer sentences (5-6 words) to communicate *e.g., "I want to ride the trike when we go outside"*	Uses more complex sentences to express ideas and feelings *e.g., "I hope we can go outside today because I want to ride the tricycle around the track"*
40. **Understands and follows oral directions**	**Forerunners** Associates words with actions *e.g., says "throw" when sees ball thrown; throws when hears the word* Follows oral directions when combined with gestures *e.g., "come here" accompanied with gesture*	Follows one-step directions *e.g., "Please get a tissue"*	Follows two-step directions *e.g., "When you get inside, please hang up your coat"*	Follows directions with more than two steps *e.g., follows directions to put clay in container, wipe table, and wash hands when activity is finished*
41. **Answers questions**	**Forerunners** Answers yes/no questions with words, gestures, or signs *e.g., points to purple paint when asked what color she wants*	Answers simple questions with one or two words *e.g., when asked for name says, "Curtis"; says, "Purple and blue" when asked the colors of paint*	Answers questions with a complete thought *e.g., responds, "I took a bus to school"; "I want purple and blue paint"*	Answers questions with details *e.g., describes a family trip when asked about weekend; says, "I want purple and blue like my new shoes so I can make lots of flowers"*
42. **Asks questions**	**Forerunners** Uses facial expressions/ gestures to ask a question Uses rising intonation to ask questions *e.g., "Mama comes back?"* Uses some "wh" words (what and where) to ask questions *e.g., "What that?"*	Asks simple questions *e.g., "What's for lunch?" "Can we play outside today?"*	Asks questions to further understanding *e.g., "Where did the snow go when it melted?" "Why does that man wear a uniform?"*	Asks increasingly complex questions to further own understanding *e.g., "What happened to the water in the fish tank? Did the fish drink it?"*

Listening and Speaking (continued)

43.	Forerunners	Responds to comments and questions from others	Responds to others' comments in a series of exchanges	Initiates and/or extends conversations for at least four exchanges
Actively participates in conversations	Initiates communication by smiling and/or eye contact			
		e.g., when one child says, "I have new shoes," shows own shoes and says, "Look at my new shoes"	e.g., makes relevant comments during a group discussion; provides more information when message is not understood	e.g., while talking with a friend, asks questions about what happened, what friend did, and shares own ideas
	Responds to social greetings			
	e.g., waves in response to "hello" or "bye-bye"			

Reading and Writing

Curriculum Objectives	Developmental Continuum for Ages 3-5			
		I	II	III
44.	Forerunners	Listens to stories being read	Participates in story time interactively	Chooses to read on own; seeks information in books; sees self as reader
Enjoys and values reading	Looks at books and pictures with an adult or another child			
		e.g., asks teacher to read favorite story; repeats refrain when familiar book is read aloud	e.g., answers questions before, during, and after read-aloud session; relates story to self; acts out familiar story with puppets	e.g., gives reasons for liking a book; looks for other books by favorite author; uses book on birds to identify egg found on nature walk
	Chooses and looks at books independently			
	Completes phrases in familiar stories			
45.	Forerunners	Knows that print carries the message	Shows general knowledge of how print works	Knows each spoken word can be written down and read
Demonstrates understanding of print concepts	Points to print on page and says, "Read this"			
		e.g., points to printed label on shelf and says, "Cars go here"; looking at the name the teacher has written on another child's drawing, says, "Whose is this?"	e.g., runs finger over text left to right, top to bottom as he pretends to read; knows that names begin with a big letter	e.g., touches a written word for every spoken word in a story; looking at a menu asks, "Which word says pancakes?"
	Recognizes logos			
	e.g., McDonald's			
	Recognizes book by cover			
46.	Forerunners	Recognizes and identifies a few letters by name	Recognizes and names many letters	Begins to make letter-sound connections
Demonstrates knowledge of the alphabet	Participates in songs and fingerplays about letters			
		e.g., points to a cereal box and says, "That's C like in my name"	e.g., uses alphabet stamps and names the letters— "D, T, M"	e.g., writes a big M and says, "This is for Mommy"
	Points out print in environment			
	e.g., name on cubby, exit sign			

47. Uses emerging reading skills to make meaning from print	**Forerunners** Uses familiar logos and words to read print *e.g., cereal logos, "exit" and "stop" signs* Recognizes own name in print and uses it as a cue to find possessions *e.g., cubby, cot, placemat*	Uses illustrations to guess what the text says *e.g., looking at* The Three Pigs, *says, "And the wolf blew down the pig's house"*	Makes judgements about words and text by noticing features (other than letters or words) *e.g., "That must be Christopher's name because it's so long"; "You didn't write enough words. I said, 'A Book about the Dog Biff,' and you just wrote three words"*	Uses different strategies (known words, knowledge of letters and sounds, patterns in text) to make meaning from print *e.g., "That word says* book"; *anticipates what comes next based on pattern in* Brown Bear; *figures out which word says* banana *because he knows it starts with* b
48. Comprehends and interprets meaning from books and other texts	**Forerunners** Repeats words and actions demonstrated in books *e.g., roars like a lion* Relates story to self and shares information *e.g., after hearing a story about snow says, "I made a snowman"*	Imitates act of reading in play *e.g., holds up book and pretends to read to baby doll; takes out phonebook in dramatic play area to make a phone call*	Compares and predicts story events; acts out main events of a familiar story *e.g., compares own feelings about baby brother to those of character; re-enacts* Three Billy Goats Gruff	Retells a story including many details and draws connections between story events *e.g., says, "The wolf blew the house down because it wasn't strong"; uses flannel board to retell* The Very Hungry Caterpillar
49. Understands the purpose of writing	**Forerunners** Watches when others write Pretends to write (scribble writes)	Imitates act of writing in play *e.g., pretends to write a prescription while playing clinic; scribble writes next to a picture*	Understands there is a way to write that conveys meaning *e.g., tells teacher, "Write this down so everyone can read it"; asks teacher, "How do I write* Happy Birthday?"; *says, "That's not writing, that's scribble-scrabble"*	Writes to convey meaning *e.g., on drawing for sick friend, writes own name; copies teacher's sign, "Do Not Disturb," to put near block pattern; makes deliberate letter choices during writing attempts*
50. Writes letters and words	**Forerunners** Scribbles with crayons Experiments with writing tools such as markers and pencils Draws simple pictures to represent something	Uses scribble writing and letter-like forms	Writes recognizable letters, especially those in own name	Uses letters that represent sounds in writing words

Taken together, the goals and objectives within these four areas of development give you a roadmap for assessing children's progress and implementing *The Creative Curriculum.*

2. Collecting Facts

The first step in the assessment process is to learn about the children you teach—what they know and can do in relation to each of the 50 *Creative Curriculum* objectives. Ongoing observation, therefore, is an essential part of connecting assessment and curriculum. To help you remember and use what you learn from your observations, you need systems to document what you see. In addition to your observation notes, you can collect concrete evidence of what children are able to do by keeping samples of their work over time and maintaining them in portfolios.

Setting Up a System

Before you begin to collect facts by observing and documenting children's learning, take the time to set up a system for taking and organizing your notes on each child. That way you can avoid finding yourself with a large collection of observation notes to sort through and organize all at once.

Systems for Taking Notes

Keep your documentation simple. If your notes are too elaborate, then you will take valuable time away from interacting with children. You don't want to feel so burdened that observation becomes a chore. Set up simple systems to make collecting observations as convenient as possible. Here are some ideas that have worked for other teachers.

- Use mailing labels or sticky notes to record your observations. At the beginning of the day, place three or four notes or labels with the names of the three or four children whom you wish to observe that day on a clipboard and keep it handy.

- Keep sticky notes in your pocket or in each interest area. Have one folder in each interest area divided into 20 squares (or whatever number represents the number of children in your class). In each square write a child's name.

- Develop your own system of shorthand so you can record information quickly. Stick to brief notes, use short phrases, and abbreviate whenever possible. You can underline particular words to indicate emphasis.

The illustration below shows what these techniques look like in practice.

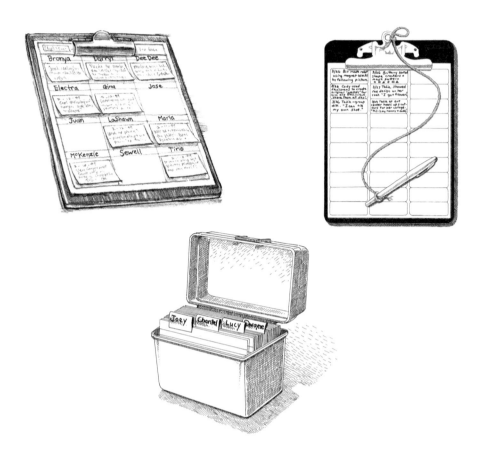

Be reassured by the fact that you don't have to write an observation on every child every day. That would be unrealistic. Try to set a goal of writing three or four brief notes a day. As a reminder to yourself, write the names of the children you plan to observe on your weekly plan so no child is overlooked. And remember, you don't need to record everything that happens and every word a child says.

A System for Organizing Your Observation Notes

Here is an approach for organizing your notes that worked well for teachers who piloted this assessment system.

1. Purchase a large looseleaf notebook and include a tabbed divider for each child in your class. In the front of the binder, place a copy of *The Creative Curriculum* Goals and Objectives at a Glance (see Appendix A) inside a plastic cover to protect it. Next, insert a copy of *The Creative Curriculum Developmental Continuum* to use as a reference.

2. Behind each tab, insert the *Individual Child Profile* form and four blank pages. At the top of each blank page, write one of these headings: social/emotional, physical, cognitive, and language development. You may want to have these printed and copied on colored paper, using a different color for each developmental area. You will store your observational notes on these pages.

To keep track of all the children in your group, write down all of their names in the spaces provided on the *Class Summary Worksheet*. Because you will be using this form almost daily, keep it in a convenient place, perhaps on a clipboard.

Once you have your system in place for taking and organizing observation notes, you can begin collecting facts by observing and documenting what you see.

Observing and Documenting Children's Learning

Observation is the basis of all good teaching and the foundation of any assessment system. Observation involves looking objectively at what a child does and says to learn about the child (Jablon, Dombro, and Dichtelmiller 1999). We suggest two strategies for recording observations: short, informal notes and more formal observations.

Short, informal notes. Most of your observations of children occur during the day as you work directly with children. In these instances, you have to take a moment and absorb the scene at hand. For example, you may find yourself in the Dramatic Play Area, checking out some items from the grocery store that's been set up. The child behind the plastic cash register takes an empty box of cereal you hand him and makes a scanning motion across the divider separating you. After "checking out," you take a moment to jot down a few notes about what you've just observed. Later on, you organize and evaluate your notes. You observe how this child is able to take on pretend roles and situations (Objective 35) and make believe with objects (Objective 36).

Formal observations. In addition to observing while you are involved with the children, try to schedule time for more formal observations—where you systematically watch one or more children and record what you see and hear. This way of observing allows you to slow down and notice things you otherwise might miss. Try to arrange for your co-teacher or a parent volunteer to be with the children so you can free yourself to do this type of observation on a daily basis.

The goals and objectives in *The Creative Curriculum* can help you focus your observations. You may wish to follow one child for a period of time and jot down behaviors you observe that relate to one goal on the *Developmental Continuum*. Or you may decide to observe a group of children playing to see where each child is with respect to one objective. Both types of observations yield rich data to help you in planning learning activities.

To think about how each child in your program is progressing, you'll want to collect observations that relate to all of the 50 objectives in the *Developmental Continuum*. This does not mean, however, that you need to conduct 50 separate observations on each child in your class. One observation can yield information about many objectives. For example, your observations of a child in the Art Area may reveal evidence of the child's progress in meeting the following objectives:

#5: Demonstrates self-direction and independence

#7: Respects and cares for classroom environment and materials

#19: Controls small muscles in hands

#20: Coordinates eye-hand movement

#21: Uses tools for writing and drawing

#24: Shows persistence in approaching tasks

#30: Recognizes patterns and can repeat them

Depending on what is taking place, you might note a child's progress on these or any number of other objectives.

Document Your Observations Accurately and Objectively

To be useful, observation notes should be objective and factual. When your notes include words like *shy, aggressive, upset, hyperactive,* or *angry,* they reveal your impressions or assumptions rather than what a child actually did or said. These judgmental words may or may not tell an accurate story of what actually took place. On the other hand, a series of objective, factual observations will eventually lead you to a useful conclusion. Along the way, you may discover something completely unexpected.

Taking objective notes requires practice. Below are two examples of objective observation notes.

Crystal *11/14*	*Derrick* *10/30*
Places two colored blocks on a pattern card correctly and continues the pattern: red/blue, r/b/r/b/r/b.	*Pounds nails into a tree stump. Says, "My Dad's building new steps on our house."*

Maintaining a Portfolio for Each Child

A portfolio is a system for organizing samples of a child's work to document progress over time. Because a portfolio is a purposeful collection, it contains such items as dated samples of a child's artwork and writing, and photographs of a child's finished work such as a completed block structure or an intricate design with pattern blocks. The items in a portfolio are concrete examples of a child's efforts, achievements, and approaches to learning. Taken together, these materials show progress over time.

Collect a Variety of Items for a Portfolio

While you don't need a large number of work samples, you do need a variety to tell you the whole story. Each sample of a child's work can reveal a great deal of information about that child's development. In the following example, 4-year-old Tasheen drew a picture on the wipe-off board. The teacher had displayed a "Please do not erase" sign for times when children wanted to preserve their work for a while. Tasheen created her own sign, using the teacher's sign as a model. By looking at this writing sample and observing Tasheen at work, the teacher sees that she:

- understands that print carries a message

- writes left-to-right and top-to-bottom

- understands the concept of a "word"

- writes her name, though the order of letters is sometimes reversed

- matches some upper- and lower-case letters (the teacher's sign was written in lower-case letters)

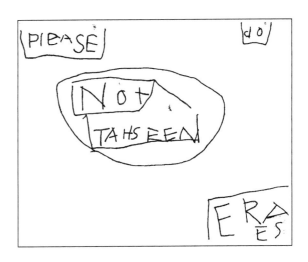

In collecting a child's work for a portfolio, be sure to write the date and a short note about what you observed because the sample alone doesn't give you all the information embedded in it. For example, it doesn't tell you that Tasheen wrote these letters from left to right or that she copied a sign; for that information you need observational notes.

To show growth, it is important to collect similar samples over a period of time. For instance, comparing a child's attempt to write her name throughout the course of the year is one excellent way to document growth. But it is hard to document growth if you compare a writing sample, a painting, a photograph of a block structure, and a dictated story. At the beginning of the year, think of two or three items—such as a writing sample or painting—that would be good for documenting growth and set a goal for yourself to collect these periodically throughout the year.

Some programs, such as CreativeCurriculum.net, use technology to collect items for a child's portfolio. For example, you can photocopy or scan children's drawings or writing samples; take photographs to capture a child's involvement in an activity or finished work; audio tape a child telling a story; or use videotapes to capture a child engaged in dramatic play or reading a book.

File the items you have collected by date and group them by areas of development—social/emotional, cognitive, language, and physical development. This will make reviewing your documentation easier when it is time to evaluate a child's progress.

3. Analyzing and Evaluating Facts

The next stage in the assessment process involves organizing your notes and making a judgment about what they tell you about a child's progress toward each of the 50 Curriculum objectives. The tools that will help you do this include:

- *The Creative Curriculum* Goals and Objectives at a Glance
- *The Creative Curriculum Developmental Continuum*
- *Class Summary Worksheet*
- *Individual Child Profile*

Two further detailed items are available separately: *The Expanded Forerunners of The Creative Curriculum Developmental Continuum for Ages 3–5* and the *Individual Child Profile—Expanded Forerunners.*

Analyzing Facts

The first step is a simple sorting task. It involves organizing your observation notes by area of development for each child. It takes very little time to do this analysis, but it will preserve your notes and make them easy to find when you need them.

At the end of each day, or at least several times a week, when you have collected a number of observation notes, take out the class looseleaf notebook you put together and:

- Put all the notes you have on one child together.
- Review the notes for one child at a time and decide what area of development the observation note relates to most: social/emotional, physical, cognitive, or language.
- Sort your notes onto the appropriate pages behind each child's name in your notebook.

On a regular basis ask yourself, "What does this mean?" Using the Goals and Objectives at a Glance, decide which objectives apply and jot down the number right on the note or on the back of a work sample. Taking the two examples of observation notes from the previous section, here's how you might analyze them.

Crystal	11/14
Places two colored blocks on a pattern card correctly and continues the pattern: red/blue, r/b/r/b/r/b.	
#30	

Derrick	10/30
Pounds nails into a tree stump. Says, "My Dad's building new steps on our house."	
#20, #39	

The observation note on Crystal was very clearly related to Objective 30, "Recognizes patterns and can repeat them." The observation note on Derrick, however, relates to more than one objective. You may have placed this note originally on the page for physical development (#20, "Coordinates eye-hand movement"), but in further analyzing it, you see it also reveals evidence of Derrick's language development (#39, "Expresses self using words and expanded sentences"). You can still leave it where it is, but when you are evaluating Derrick's progress, you will use this note for both objectives.

Evaluating Children's Progress

Evaluating children's progress means deciding which step best describes each child's development for all 50 objectives. To do this you first need to gather and reflect upon all the documentation you have collected. This would include your observation notes and the child's portfolio. Now, using the *Developmental Continuum,* the *Class Summary Worksheet,* and the *Individual Child Profile,* you can begin evaluating each child's progress.

Think about what the child did and said. Decide which of the steps best represents the child's skill level for the objective.

How to Use the *Class Summary Worksheet*

Consider the *Class Summary Worksheet* as a day-to-day working document on which you can make preliminary judgments about each child's progress and track the group as a whole at the same time. The *Worksheet* can help guide your observations, and help you to consider small group and program planning needs.

While you note children's progress on the *Class Summary Worksheet* on a regular basis, there are three times during the year when you should pinpoint where each child is on each objective. We call these periods *checkpoints.* In most programs, this checkpoint is done about six weeks after school starts, at mid-year, and six weeks before school ends. (If your program operates year-round, you may want to plan for a checkpoint every four months.)

Don't wait until the last week before a checkpoint to begin using the *Class Summary Worksheet*. When you have collected several observations and samples of the children's work and have time to evaluate what you are learning about each child, begin making preliminary markings. Perhaps the children were walking across a balance beam outside today. At the end of the day you might want to consult the *Developmental Continuum* and think about your observations. Which objectives might you now have some information about? You can consider your new observations in light of previous ones to make sure your judgment is accurate.

Similarly, as you use the *Class Summary Worksheet* regularly you will notice interests or strengths on which you can build to help children reach the next developmental step. Or you may find for example, that you have not observed children outdoors for gross motor objectives. A glance at the *Worksheet* can remind you to do that this week. If you were to notice that most children are at the Forerunner level or Step I for a particular objective you could then consider changes to your environment or program to give them more opportunities to work on a particular objective.

In this way you begin to get a picture of where each child is developmentally and the progress of the group as a whole. Seeing this information for the entire group alerts you to focus your observations with certain objectives in mind, either because you have no documentation or you suspect a child needs extra help.

Before you begin to use the *Class Summary Worksheet*, choose three different color pens or pencils to distinguish your marks for the fall, winter, and spring observation checkpoints. In the fall, you might begin using pencil marks (dots or checks) and then, when you feel surer of your analysis, switch to the color for fall. During the winter you might initially make pencil marks again and then confirm with the color pencil you have chosen for winter. By the end of the year you would have three different color marks for each objective for each child. Some boxes might have more than one color mark in it if a child stayed at the same developmental step for two observation periods or regressed during an observation period. The space at the bottom for checkpoint totals allows you to keep track of the progress of your group of children. This is an important step if you are required to track your class's progress for administrators or funders.

One page of a *Class Summary Worksheet* that has been filled in for a year is included on the inside back cover of this manual.

Let's see how to begin using the *Class Summary Worksheet* with the observation note on Crystal. Looking at the *Developmental Continuum*, you decide that Crystal is at the first developmental step: Notices and recreates simple patterns with objects. On the *Class Summary Worksheet*, you put a check or dot under Objective 30, step I.

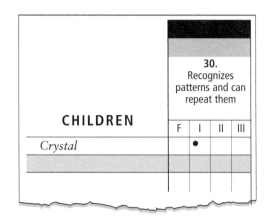

An example from a *Class Summary Worksheet*.

When the checkpoint period comes, you gather all the documentation you have collected, your *Class Summary Worksheet*, and the *Developmental Continuum*. Now look at your last marking for that objective on the *Class Summary Worksheet*. Was your mark appropriate, or do you need to adjust it?

How to Use the *Individual Child Profile*

Between checkpoints you will find that it is easier to maintain up-to-date information using the *Class Summary Worksheet*. However, at each checkpoint, it is appropriate to enter your marks on the *Individual Child Profile*. This will be your way to record the developmental progress of each child at three checkpoints during the year. This form can become part of the child's permanent records to help next year's teachers see what the child can do.

Review multiple observation notes and portfolio items before making a decision about each objective. As you do so, you may sometimes find that the child's behavior corresponds to more than one step. These guidelines will help you to select the appropriate step of the objective:

- Select the step that describes the child's behavior or skill level most consistently. Remember that the examples offered for each step are only sample behaviors.

You may observe behavior related to an objective that is different from the examples provided.

- If a child is just beginning to exhibit skills for a step, place the child at the previous step.

- Look at the dates on the observation notes and portfolio items. If notes taken early in the checkpoint period indicate a lower step than notes taken later, and if the child consistently exhibits skills at a higher step now, choose the higher step.

Evaluate each child's development on all 50 objectives in this way. While a child's skill level is likely to be the same for many objectives, children may be more advanced in one developmental area than another. For example, a particular child may be at Step 1 for one objective and Step 2 for another. Children identified with developmental delays or disabilities may require the use of *The Expanded Forerunners of The Creative Curriculum Developmental Continuum for Ages 3–5* to show progress at the Forerunner level.

For your information to be useful, all teachers in the program must assess children in the same way. Follow this strategy to establish interrater reliability:

- Review the goals, objectives, and steps of the *Developmental Continuum* with all teachers. Review the process of ongoing assessment that includes collecting, analyzing, and then evaluating facts. Make sure all teachers understand how to choose the step that best reflects the child's development.

- Have pairs of teachers observe the same child and then compare their observation notes to make sure they present facts without interpreting them.

- Collect a set of observation notes and portfolio samples and review them as a team for consistency.

- Repeat this process until the teaching team agrees about how to choose the steps that best describe the child's development.

When you are ready to transfer this information to the *Individual Child Profile* form, it will look like this.

LOGICAL THINKING (continued)		CHECKPOINT	
	F	W	S
30. Recognizes patterns and can repeat them	F	W	S
Forerunner examples:			
I Notices and recreates simple patterns with objects	✓		
II Extends patterns or creates simple patterns of own design			
III Creates complex patterns of own design or by copying			

An example from an *Individual Child Profile* form.

4. Planning for Each Child and the Group

This step in the assessment process is what makes all the work of collecting, analyzing, and evaluating children's progress worthwhile. The wealth of information you have on each child, and your group as a whole, is only meaningful if it is used to make decisions, to plan for each child, and to plan for your group of children. The link between curriculum and assessment becomes clear at this stage.

Using What You Learn to Make Decisions

Teachers make many decisions each day as they observe children and respond to them based on what they feel the child needs to extend learning. Often your observations lead you to ask questions as you reflect on what you learn about a child and consider how best to provide support. Here are some examples of the kinds of questions your observations may lead you to ask.

- Tyrone needs help in learning to play with other children (Objective 10). His approach to joining a group leads the other children to reject him. How can I teach him a more successful way to be accepted? Who might become his friend?

- Susie imitates simple actions with the play telephone in the Dramatic Play Area (Objective 35). How can I help her move to the next step—using the phone to make a call as part of her play?

- Derrick has just learned to recognize the first letter of his name (Objective 46). How can I provide more opportunities for him to see his name used in a variety of ways and places throughout the day and help him focus on this?

When you determine a child's developmental step on the *Continuum* as described in the previous chapter, you can then decide what support a child needs to move to the next step. For example, with Crystal you might ask yourself, "How can I help her to extend patterns or create patterns of her own design?" Here's what you might do.

While working with Crystal in the Toys and Games Area, you watch her making a tower of interlocking cubes—red, white, red, white. To help Crystal move from working with simple patterns to ones that are more complex, you pick up another set of cubes and begin making a pattern using three colors. You say to Crystal, "What am I doing with my cubes?" Crystal replies, "You've got red, white, blue, red, white, blue, red, and white." You ask, "What comes next?" Crystal answers, "Blue." You then encourage her to add blue cubes to her structure.

Over the next few days, you notice that Crystal is beginning to work on more complex patterns. To further support Crystal's learning about patterns, you draw her attention to patterns in the environment. On the playground, you help Crystal observe a pattern in the fence and the design in the hedges. Gradually, Crystal starts making more complicated patterns both with table toys and in music.

As this example illustrates, the *Developmental Continuum* is a powerful tool for helping you to identify where a child is in relation to each curriculum objective and how to support the next step in development. Because it covers all areas of development, using the *Continuum* gives you a comprehensive picture of the whole child.

Planning for Each Child Using the *Child Progress and Planning Report*

The main purpose of summarizing each child's progress at three points during the year is to share this information with families and jointly plan how best to support the child's development and learning. Plan on meeting formally with each child's parents at least three times a year, at each summary period. The first meeting is a time to get to know each other, to share information you each have about the child, and to discuss in greater detail your goals for the year. If you prepare for these conferences, you will feel more at ease.

Preparing for a Conference

Before meeting with families, go through the child's portfolio and the binder to be sure everything is up to date. Look over your observation notes and the samples of work you have collected, and think about what they tell you about the child's progress. Review what you have learned about each child as documented on the *Class Summary Worksheet* and the *Individual Child Profile*. What does it tell you about the child's social and emotional skills? Fine and gross motor skills? Cognitive development? Language skills?

This gives you a picture of the child's level in all areas of development. Now you use the *Child Progress and Planning Report* to begin planning. The first section of this form is called "Summary of Developmental Progress." Here you can summarize what you have learned about a child's development based on your observations and analysis. The four boxes on this form correspond to each of the four areas of development. In each box, we list the Curriculum goals. The *Individual Child Profile* gives you more than enough information to highlight those accomplishments you feel are significant and likely to be of most interest to each child's family.

A final step in preparing for the conference is to give some thought to what are the next steps for this child, and what strategies will you discuss with the child's family. Ask yourself, "What skills and knowledge does this child need in order to pursue his/her interests? How can I build on this child's interests and strengths?" You won't have all the answers before meeting with families, but you will have some ideas to offer as a starting point.

Sharing Information and Planning Together

A good way to put families at ease is to begin a conference by sharing samples of work you have collected over time. Seeing evidence—such as photos of block structures the child has made, writing samples, drawings, and dictated stories—is a concrete way to begin talking about the child's learning. Take time to explain a little about each work sample and what it tells you about the child's interests and strengths. Show parents progress their child has made by comparing earlier samples with more current ones, for example, a child's attempt at writing his name in the fall and in the winter. Most important, share something positive about the child that shows you really know what's unique and special about that child and that you really care.

Next, review what you have written summarizing the child's progress. Highlight the child's strengths as well as any areas of concern, and share specific examples from your observation notes or the child's work samples.

Invite families to share their own observations. Questions such as the following encourage families to share their perspective:

- How are things going from your point of view?
- Does your child look forward to coming to the program/school?
- What changes have you seen?
- Does your child have any special interests we should know about?
- What are you most hoping your child will learn this year?

Record what you learn in the section marked "Family Comments and Observations."

The last section of the *Progress and Planning Report* has a place to write the strategies you will use to support each child's learning. Based on the information you and the family exchange during your meeting, you can jointly develop a plan for the child. Give examples of what you plan to do at school.

Next, find out what the child's family is most comfortable doing that would help the child make progress on specific objectives. List several activities they can do at home. You may need to offer assistance by lending materials or providing guidance if the families request help. Keep your suggestions to a minimum and make them easy to implement. Think about what is most important. For example, if literacy skills are high on a parent's list and you also feel work in this area would help the child, then you might suggest the following ideas:

- Read together every day and talk together about the story and the pictures.

- Point out the labels on food containers and in signs.

- Look through pictures in magazines and ask your child questions: What do you think is happening here? How do you think this person is feeling? Can you find the orange on this page?

- Encourage your child to draw and write.

Provide families with a copy of the plan so it becomes a true blueprint for supporting the child's development and learning. When you meet next, you and the family will assess how the plan worked, review more evidence of the child's progress, and develop a new plan.

THE CREATIVE CURRICULUM®
FOR PRESCHOOL
Child Progress and Planning Report

Child's Name: _Jocelyn Jones_   Date: _3-1-01_

Teacher(s): _Ms. Frome_   Family Member(s): _Mr. Jones_

Summary of Developmental Progress:

SOCIAL/EMOTIONAL

Sense of Self; Responsibility for Self and Others; Prosocial Behavior

- *Plays well with other children, especially her best friend Rosa*
- *Recognizes the feelings of others and often offers to help them*
- *Takes care of our materials when reminded*
- *Stands up for her rights*
- *Joins in group-time activities, especially singing*

COGNITIVE

Learning and Problem Solving; Logical Thinking; Representation and Symbolic Thinking

- *Takes the lead in pretend play and uses her imagination and creativity*
- *Uses problem-solving skills to figure out how things work*
- *Understands positional words like under, over, behind, through*
- *Arranges objects from largest to smallest*
- *Classifies and sorts objects such as plastic animals*

PHYSICAL

Gross Motor; Fine Motor

- *Uses her hands well to draw, build, and create with clay*
- *Walks on balance beam, crawls, skips, and hops during game of Follow the Leader*
- *Throws and catches beanbags and medium-size balls*
- *Joins in movement activities during group time*

LANGUAGE

Listening and Speaking; Reading and Writing

- *Enjoys story time and often acts out her favorite ones*
- *Follows 2- and 3-step directions*
- *Writes many letters, including those in her name*
- *Writes or copies signs during play*
- *Enjoys playing with words; made up song "Ring-Around-the Rosa"*

FAMILY COMMENTS AND OBSERVATIONS:

- *Talks about her "best friend" Rosa at home*
- *Likes to play outside; asked older sister to teach her how to jump rope*
- *Counts everything, but sometimes gets mixed up*
- *Plays school with her sister and tries to write her ABCs*

NEXT STEPS AT SCHOOL AND AT HOME:

At school:
- *Read stories that Jocelyn can act out*
- *Help her with counting skills during play*
- *Encourage her interest in writing by showing her how to make books*

At home:
- *Read a story to Jocelyn every day*
- *Encourage her to join in saying familiar parts*
- *Encourage Jocelyn to touch objects as she counts them*

Teacher(s) Signature: _Brenda Frome_   Family Member(s) Signature: _Claudia Jones_

©2002 Teaching Strategies, Inc., PO Box 42243, Washington, DC 20015, www.TeachingStrategies.com

Planning for a Group of Children

Just as you plan for individual children, you need to plan for the whole group. You may find after summarizing progress for your group that work on some skills could benefit everyone and that you can build on other skills children have acquired. Activities take place each day in large- and small-group settings, so keep in mind what content you'd like to work on with the group. You'll also find that planning for the group extends over into the play that children do on their own.

Using What You Learn from the *Class Summary Worksheet*

When you complete your *Class Summary Worksheet*, you have a picture of the progress of your class as a whole. At a glance, you can see the strengths of your children and the areas that need further development. Use this information to make plans.

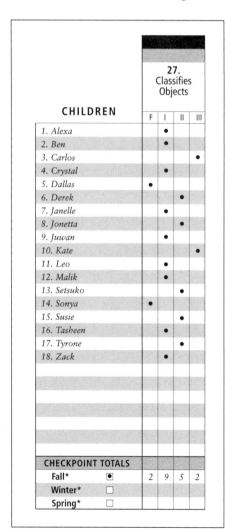

An example from a *Class Summary Worksheet*.

To illustrate how this might work, let's examine a *Class Summary Worksheet* that lists 18 children. For objective 27, Classifies objects, these 4- to 5-year-olds look like this:

- Two children are at the forerunner level. They can group similar kinds of items together, but not sort them by characteristics.

- Nine children can sort objects by one property.

- Five children can sort objects by two properties.

- Two children can sort objects into categories that they themselves determine.

If you were to reflect on what this means, you would likely conclude that while two children are at the top developmental step in classifying objects, the majority of children are still developing this skill. Therefore, classification is a skill you might wish to work on with all of the children.

To make this learning objective a group focus, you might try the following strategies:

- Stock the Toys and Games Area with lotto games, beads, and manipulatives that focus on classification skills.

- Have a parent volunteer lead a small group of children in a lotto game that uses classification skills.

- Make sure that there are collections and natural materials that children can use to classify.

- Take nature walks and bring back leaves and other objects that children can use to classify.

- Make graphs that require children to categorize objects.

- Use categorizations during transitions: "Will all the children who are wearing red **and** have Velcro fasteners on their shoes, go put on their coats."

- During group time, have children come up with different categories for recycling trash. Then label the receptacles accordingly and have children use them.

- Have children come up with categories for labeling prop boxes used in Dramatic Play and for Cooking.

The *Class Summary Worksheet* information enables you to identify those children about whom you need more information, or who would benefit from more focused practice and instruction in a particular skill. For example, you may find that you are unable to say whether five of the children can hear and discriminate the sounds of language. To find out, you plan a time to gather these children, perhaps two at a time, to read poetry and sing rhymes together. Based on what you learn, you might decide to set up some small-group activities with those children who are having trouble hearing the sounds in words.

Please keep in mind that the *Developmental Continuum* applies to children ages 3 to 5, and to children who are not at a typical level of development. Therefore, you cannot expect that every child in your program will progress to the higher levels for each objective. Similarly, in a group of 3- to 4-year-old children, you can't expect that all children will progress to the top developmental step. Over the course of the year, however, you would hope to see evidence of progress in every child.

As you can see, assessment and curriculum planning are an ongoing process. You collect facts, analyze and evaluate what they tell you about the child's development, then summarize what you learn and use the information to plan for each child and for a group of children. You then implement your plans, continue to observe and document what children do, and the cycle goes on. This is how curriculum and assessment are linked together in a *Creative Curriculum* classroom.

The Year at a Glance

September	**OBSERVATION AND DOCUMENTATION**	Observe and document; sort notes; use the *Class Summary Worksheet* to keep track of what you learn.
October		**1st Checkpoint**—Complete *Class Summary Worksheet* and *Individual Child Profiles*; complete *Child Progress and Planning Report* and meet with families.*
November		
December		Observe and document; sort notes; use the *Class Summary Worksheet* to keep track of what you learn.
January		**2nd Checkpoint**—Complete *Class Summary Worksheet* and *Individual Child Profiles*; complete *Child Progress and Planning Report* and meet with families.*
February		
March		Observe and document; sort notes; use the *Class Summary Worksheet* to keep track of what you learn.
April		**3rd Checkpoint**—Complete *Class Summary Worksheet* and *Individual Child Profiles*; complete *Child Progress and Planning Report* and meet with families.*
May		

* If you are using CC-PORT™ to report outcomes, enter data at this time.

5. Using Technology to Analyze and Report on Group Progress

Information on children's progress will be of interest to several groups. Teachers and administrators can use this information to evaluate the effectiveness of the program and determine any needed changes. Increasingly, early childhood programs are being mandated to demonstrate that children are making progress and acquiring the skills needed to be successful in school. One source of data for generating outcomes reports is the information teachers have collected on individual children and then summarized for the group. Programs that have an assessment system tied to their curriculum should have no trouble gathering and analyzing information and reporting outcomes.

The Creative Curriculum Progress and Outcomes Reporting Tool

The task of preparing reports is easily done using the software program *The Creative Curriculum Progress and Outcomes Reporting Tool* (CC-PORT™). (Programs which have large numbers of children, or multiple site locations, or which are interested in maximizing the planning potential of their information, may be interested in exploring CreativeCurriculum.net—the comprehensive, online subscription service that replicates and extends the capacities of the *Toolkit* and CC-PORT™.) CC-PORT™ is available on a CD-ROM and uses the information you collect using the *Developmental Continuum* Assessment System. It allows you to compare the progress of a group of children in several categories, depending on the information you need and type of reports you are required to produce. By using CC-PORT™, you can create a report that includes a narrative, tables, and charts illustrating the percentage of children at each developmental step in the fall, winter, and spring. For example, it will show you what progress your group of children has made in each of *The Creative Curriculum* developmental areas—social/emotional, physical, cognitive, and language. You can also see where your group of children is in relation to eight widely recognized categories that will help programs analyze information and answer questions about children's progress in language, literacy, mathematics, science, creative arts, approaches to learning, social/emotional development, and physical health and development. In addition, legislative mandates require Head Start programs to report on group progress related to 13 specific categories, called domain elements and indicators.

Key to Head Start Domain Elements and Indicators

1. Understands an increasingly complex and varied vocabulary.

2. Develops increasing abilities to understand and use language to communicate information, experiences, ideas, feelings, opinions, needs, questions, and for other varied purposes.

3. For non-English-speaking children, progresses in listening to and understanding English.*

4. Uses an increasingly complex and varied spoken vocabulary.

5. For non-English-speaking children, progresses in speaking English.*

6. Phonological awareness.

7. Associates sounds with written words.

8. Book knowledge and appreciation.

9. Print awareness and concepts.

10. Recognizes a word as a unit of print.

11. Identifies at least 10 letters of the alphabet, especially those in their own name.

12. Knows that letters of the alphabet are a special category of visual graphics that can be individually named.

13. Number and operations.

Following this page is a chart that shows how each of *The Creative Curriculum for Preschool* objectives relates to all of these categories.

---

* Please note, for children whose first language is not English, the *Developmental Continuum* does not assess a child's progress toward acquisition of English. Therefore, this reporting tool does not provide information about progress in this area.

Alignment of *The Creative Curriculum® for Preschool* and the Head Start Child Outcomes Framework

	Language	Literacy	Mathematics	Science	Creative Arts	Approaches to Learning	Social/Emotional Development	Physical Health & Well Being	1	2	3	4	5	6	7	8	9	10	11	12	13
SOCIAL/EMOTIONAL DEVELOPMENT																					
Sense of Self																					
1. Shows ability to adjust to new situations							●														
2. Demonstrates appropriate trust in adults							●														
3. Recognizes own feelings and manages them appropriately	●				●		●			●											
4. Stands up for rights	●						●			●											
Responsibility for Self and Others																					
5. Demonstrates self-direction and independence							●	●													
6. Takes responsibility for own well-being							●	●													
7. Respects and cares for classroom environment and materials						●	●														
8. Follows classroom routines							●	●													
9. Follows classroom rules							●	●													
Prosocial Behavior																					
10. Plays well with other children							●														
11. Recognizes the feelings of others and responds appropriately							●														
12. Shares and respects the rights of others							●														
13. Uses thinking skills to resolve conflicts	●						●														
PHYSICAL DEVELOPMENT																					
Gross Motor																					
14. Demonstrates basic locomotor skills (running, jumping, hopping, galloping)								●													
15. Shows balance while moving					●			●													
16. Climbs up and down								●													

13 Domain Elements & Indicators (See Key for Descriptions)

Alignment of *The Creative Curriculum* for Preschool and the Head Start Child Outcomes Framework

	Language	Literacy	Mathematics	Science	Creative Arts	Approaches to Learning	Social/Emotional Development	Physical Health & Well Being	1	2	3	4	5	6	7	8	9	10	11	12	13
														13 Domain Elements & Indicators (See Key for Descriptions)							
17. Pedals and steers a tricycle (or other wheeled vehicle)								●													
18. Demonstrates throwing, kicking, and catching skills								●													
Fine Motor																					
19. Controls small muscles in hands		●						●													
20. Coordinates eye-hand movement		●						●													
21. Uses tools for writing and drawing				●	●			●													
COGNITIVE DEVELOPMENT																					
Learning and Problem Solving																					
22. Observes objects and events with curiosity				●		●															
23. Approaches problems flexibly			●	●		●															●
24. Shows persistence in approaching tasks						●															
25. Explores cause and effect				●		●															
26. Applies knowledge or experience to a new context						●															
Logical Thinking																					
27. Classifies objects			●	●		●															●
28. Compares/measures			●	●		●															●
29. Arranges objects in a series			●			●															●
30. Recognizes patterns and can repeat them	●		●		●	●															●
31. Shows awareness of time concepts and sequence			●	●																	●
32. Shows awareness of position in space			●	●	●			●													●
33. Uses one-to-one correspondence			●																		●
34. Uses numbers and counting			●																		●
Representation and Symbolic Thinking																					
35. Takes on pretend roles and situations		●			●					●						●					
36. Makes believe with objects					●															●	
37. Makes and interprets representations	●	●	●		●	●											●				●

Alignment of *The Creative Curriculum® for Preschool* and the Head Start Child Outcomes Framework

	Language	Literacy	Mathematics	Science	Creative Arts	Approaches to Learning	Social/Emotional Development	Physical Health & Well Being	13 Domain Elements & Indicators (See Key for Descriptions)												
									1	2	3	4	5	6	7	8	9	10	11	12	13
LANGUAGE DEVELOPMENT																					
Listening and Speaking																					
38. Hears and discriminates the sounds of language	●	●			●									●	●						
39. Expresses self using words and expanded sentences	●	●					●			●	●	●									
40. Understands and follows oral directions	●								●												
41. Answers questions	●					●			●	●											
42. Asks questions	●					●				●		●									
43. Actively participates in conversations	●																				
Reading and Writing																					
44. Enjoys and values reading		●														●					
45. Demonstrates understanding of print concepts		●														●		●		●	
46. Demonstrates knowledge of the alphabet		●												●	●		●	●	●	●	
47. Uses emerging reading skills to make meaning from print		●													●		●	●	●	●	
48. Comprehends and interprets meaning from books and other texts	●	●						●	●							●					
49. Understands the purpose of writing		●																●	●	●	
50. Writes letters and words		●																●	●	●	

Conclusion

As you have seen in this Guide, assessment and curriculum are so closely linked that they should not be separated. Assessing children's progress in the context of everyday activities informs the decisions you make in planning for individuals and groups. We have shown you how to *collect facts* through observation and documentation; how to *analyze and evaluate* children's progress using *The Developmental Continuum*; and how to *plan* instruction *for each child and the group* based on what you have learned. In addition, we have demonstrated a way to report outcomes on groups of children and how to use that information to improve your program. We have also referred you to two technological extensions of the *Toolkit,* CC-PORT™ and CreativeCurriculum.net, and to *The Expanded Forerunners of The Creative Curriculum Developmental Continuum for Ages 3–5* for children identified with developmental delays or disabilities. We hope that this assessment system will help you take a close look at each child's unique abilities, interests, and needs. Using this system, you will have a wealth of information to promote each child's successful learning and to implement *The Creative Curriculum* effectively.

Appendices

Appendix A

Appendix B

The Creative Curriculum® Goals and Objectives at a Glance

SOCIAL/EMOTIONAL DEVELOPMENT

Sense of Self

1. Shows ability to adjust to new situations
2. Demonstrates appropriate trust in adults
3. Recognizes own feelings and manages them appropriately
4. Stands up for rights

Responsibility for Self and Others

5. Demonstrates self-direction and independence
6. Takes responsibility for own well-being
7. Respects and cares for classroom environment and materials
8. Follows classroom routines
9. Follows classroom rules

Prosocial Behavior

10. Plays well with other children
11. Recognizes the feelings of others and responds appropriately
12. Shares and respects the rights of others
13. Uses thinking skills to resolve conflicts

PHYSICAL DEVELOPMENT

Gross Motor

14. Demonstrates basic locomotor skills (running, jumping, hopping, galloping)
15. Shows balance while moving
16. Climbs up and down
17. Pedals and steers a tricycle (or other wheeled vehicle)
18. Demonstrates throwing, kicking, and catching skills

Fine Motor

19. Controls small muscles in hands
20. Coordinates eye-hand movement
21. Uses tools for writing and drawing

COGNITIVE DEVELOPMENT

Learning and Problem Solving

22. Observes objects and events with curiosity
23. Approaches problems flexibly
24. Shows persistence in approaching tasks
25. Explores cause and effect
26. Applies knowledge or experience to a new context

Logical Thinking

27. Classifies objects
28. Compares/measures
29. Arranges objects in a series
30. Recognizes patterns and can repeat them
31. Shows awareness of time concepts and sequence
32. Shows awareness of position in space
33. Uses one-to-one correspondence
34. Uses numbers and counting

Representation and Symbolic Thinking

35. Takes on pretend roles and situations
36. Makes believe with objects
37. Makes and interprets representations

LANGUAGE DEVELOPMENT

Listening and Speaking

38. Hears and discriminates the sounds of language
39. Expresses self using words and expanded sentences
40. Understands and follows oral directions
41. Answers questions
42. Asks questions
43. Actively participates in conversations

Reading and Writing

44. Enjoys and values reading
45. Demonstrates understanding of print concepts
46. Demonstrates knowledge of the alphabet
47. Uses emerging reading skills to make meaning from print
48. Comprehends and interprets meaning from books and other texts
49. Understands the purpose of writing
50. Writes letters and words

Looking at the Objectives and the Expanded Forerunners

The following illustration shows how the Expanded Forerunners describe sequential developmental steps within the Forerunner level for each objective.

Developmental Continuum for Ages 3–5

Curriculum Objectives	Forerunner 1	Forerunner 2	Forerunner 3	Step I
1. **Shows ability to adjust to new situations**	Watches classroom activities with family member *e.g., stands behind family member and observes other children*	Engages in classroom activities when family member is nearby *e.g., goes to another part of the room with teacher, checking back occasionally to see family member*	Engages in classroom activities with support of familiar staff member *e.g., says good-bye to parent and joins activity but may still show distress for a time; joins activity with teacher but looks toward door through which parent left*	Treats arrival and departure as routine parts of the day *e.g., says good-bye to family members without undue stress; accepts comfort from teacher*

The three shaded boxes below the long arrow are labeled *Forerunner 1*, *Forerunner 2*, and *Forerunner 3*. They describe points of emerging skill development before Step I of the particular objective. Step I approximates a beginning level of development typical of children ages 3–5. For Objective 1, "Shows ability to adjust to new situations," Forerunner 1 is "Watches classroom activities with family member." An example of what a child might do at this Forerunner step is stand behind a family member to observe other children.

The next description of emergent behavior that relates to this objective is Forerunner 2: "Engages in classroom activities when family member is nearby." For example, a child at the Forerunner 2 step might go to another part of the room with a teacher, checking back occasionally to see a family member.

A more advanced level of skill development is Forerunner 3: "Engages in classroom activities with support of familiar staff member." An example that illustrates this Forerunner step is a child who joins an activity with a familiar teacher but looks toward the door through which his parent left.

References

The Child Mental Health Foundations and Agencies Network. 2000. *A Good Beginning: Sending America's Children to School with the Social and Emotional Competence They Need to Succeed.* Bethesda, MD: The National Institute of Mental Health.

International Reading Association and the National Council of Teachers of English. 1996. *Standards for the English Language Arts.* Newark, DE: International Reading Association.

Jablon, J.R., A.L. Dombro, and M.L. Dichtelmiller. 1999. *The Power of Observation.* Washington, DC: Teaching Strategies, Inc.

National Institute of Child Health and Human Development. 2000. *Report of the National Reading Panel: Teaching Children to Read: An Evidence-Based Assessment of the Scientific Research Literature on Reading and Its Implications for Reading Instruction.* Washington, DC: National Institute of Child Health and Human Development, National Institutes of Health.

National Research Council. 1998. *Preventing Reading Difficulties in Young Children.* Washington, DC: National Academy Press.

National Research Council. 1999. *Starting Out Right: A Guide to Promoting Children's Reading Success.* Washington, DC: National Academy Press.

Neuman, S. B., C. Copple, and S. Bredekamp. 2000. *Learning to Read and Write: Developmentally Appropriate Practices for Young Children.* Washington, DC: NAEYC.

A Report of the Surgeon General. 1996. *Physical Activity and Health.* Washington, DC: U.S. Department of Health and Human Services.